In the Pursuit of Happiness: Finding It Hard

by J.P. Hope

Dedicated to all those who are struggling

You are not alone

You are worthy

You are strong

You are courageous

There's nothing that you haven't survived

You will get through this

Hold on

Dark Place

In the depths of despair, where pitch darkness looms,
And the weight of the world feels like heavy tombs,
Have hope, my dear soul, for this is not the end,
But start of a journey, right around the bend.

For just as flowers push through the soil's embrace,
To reach for the sun, with unwavering grace,
You'll surmount and rise up, continue your fight,
To breathe in the fresh air and to find the light.

Though the path may seem not to lead anywhere,
And burdens you carry, too heavy to bear,
Know that within you lies a great strength untold,
A resilience that is destined to unfold.

For in the darkest of nights, the stars still shine,
Guiding you on your way with their bold design.
And though the climb is steep, the road may be long,
Each step takes you closer to where you belong.

So hold onto hope, dear, let it steer you right,
For even in darkness, it shines ever bright.
And know that this moment, though with some pain fraught,
Is just the first step to the relief you have sought.

For you were not buried, merely planted deep,
Like a seed in the soil of life, you will leap.
Just as the flowers bloom from the earth's embrace,
When you rise, you will do so with newfound grace.

So push through the darkness, let hope be your guide,
For on the other side, this steep slope's a slide.
The challenges you face are but stepping stones,
To the life you deserve, to the seeds you've sown.

Only In Darkness

In the black depths of night, where the shadows rule,
Better in darkness can you see the light's pull.
In view of the absence of the sun's bright glow,
The faintest spark's glimmer is a radiant show.

When you feel the bottom underneath your feet,
Weighed down with great pressure, it is not defeat.
What you need to do is, your strengths to convene,
Use them to push you up, just like trampoline.

With dark stormy clouds looming over your head,
Look closely for the silver lining instead,
That's the sun peeking out, let it be your guide,
Your beacon as you will journey far and wide.

If you have lost the map and with it your way,
When all seems lost to you, and hope fades away,
Without the misguided directions in mind,
Finally, your own way and path can you find.

When the wind starts blowing straight up in your face,
With a strength so big that you can't stay in place,
Use its force in favour of you, fill your sails,
And with it you power on your chosen trails.

Crack

If life has let you down, and the skies are grey,
When you're feeling broken and just not okay,
Do not be discouraged, for in every crack,
Opportunity lies for light to sneak back.

Allow the sun's glimmer to peek through the tears,
Light up the way forward, calming all your fears.
For in every fracture, and in every chink,
Is a chance to flourish, a chance to rethink.

We're broken, not shattered, and we still stand tall,
Perfectly imperfect, each one and us all.
And in these crevices, seeds of strength are sown,
Each crack a reminder that we're not alone.

For it's through our defects that beauty shines bright,
Through a path of struggles, our souls find the light.
Let's look through the crevice and try to find glee,
For it's through our broken, that we truly see.

Beautifully Broken

Ceramics broken and repaired with gold,
More valuable still, their worth will unfold.
For in the mending, can beauty arise,
A tale of resilience, strength that defies.

With delicate movements, the fractures in build,
With shimmering gold dust, each crevice is skilled.
A true masterpiece now, to behold a sight,
In the wake of its fall, a wrong is made right.

As in being broken, transpires a chance,
For metamorphosis, to neatly advance.
For what was once shattered is now standing tall,
Uniquely superior, refusing to fall.

So cherish the broken, the scars that remain,
For they tell a story, of courage through pain.
A phoenix reborn, the message is clear.
A symbol of triumph, overcoming fear.

GET UP
DOWN

Accident vs Choice

Fell down? An accident, it's true,
But staying down, that's up to you.
When life is harsh, and darkness looms,
Have the power to rise from gloom.

In case of trouble, do stand tall,
You have the strength to conquer all.
Though stumbling blocks may come your way,
You choose to rise up, come what may.

With every setback, lessons learn,
And with each fall, resilience earn.
Don't let failure define your fate,
For staying down is not that great.

So choose to rise, and choose to fight,
Do not give up, this is not right.
And though the way uphill may be,
The best of views are not for free.

If you stumble, and even fall,
Go on, persist, give it your all.
For there is no reward so sweet,
As having reached your goal complete.

ANGER

Holding onto anger is to drink poison and,
Expect the other person to thus meet their end.
It is your own joy you seize, when anger burns within,
A soul-consuming fire, right underneath your skin.

Even if you both drink it, with the cup in your hand,
It's your own fate you're holding, that you must understand.
So if inside is anger, you have to let it go,
And grab a hold of kindness, only then you can grow.

So let go of resentment, release the chains that bind,
For it is in forgiveness, that true freedom you'll find.
Forgive not for their sake, but your own peace of mind,
As you cannot move forward, 'til you leave rage behind.

So let the goodness in you, all negatives replace,
And choose the path of love, compassion, and of grace.
At last, having found your peace, you set your spirit free,
To soar above all the pain, to where you're meant to be.

Provoked

Sometimes you mirror how others treat you,
Because their actions can make you feel blue.
Mistreated, provoked, don't know what to say,
While at your armour they still chip away.

With every harsh word, every unkind deed,
Your spirit falters, your heart starts to bleed.
For you are human, with emotions raw,
Yet have to withstand every unfair blow.

Now please bear in mind, you are not defined,
By others' actions, or their words unkind.
You are resilient, your strength burns within,
The battles you face with courage - a win.

Your armor may chip and cracks may appear,
Your worth remains firm, though, your conscience clear.
For it's in your stance, grace under fire,
That your essence shines, reaching much higher.

So hold your head high, you will be alright,
For you are much more than battles you fight.
Your worth now affirmed, from conflict you rise,
Dignity intact, against all the lies.

Feel It

Feel the feeling, don't become it,
In the sea of emotions, gently sit.
Witness the waves of sensation rise,
Allow them to flow, beneath the skies.

In that still moment, don't do, just be,
Let the emotions pass, wild and free.
Release the grip of turmoil's hold,
As the rivers of feelings gently unfold.

In the languid dance of heart and mind,
Let go of the need to grasp or find.
Embrace the ebb and flow of tide,
As sensation in their beauty glide.

Feel what's inside you, let it flow,
In the depths of emotion, gently row.
Witness, allow, release the sea,
As only then will you break free.

COCOON (IN BETWEEN)

Cocooned and uncertain, here I find myself,
No more caterpillar, not yet butterfly,
Caught between the two worlds, like stuck on a shelf,
Such yearning to transform, but afraid to fly.

Can anyone hear me, searching high and low,
For I know not what I am now to do.
I need to surrender, I need to let go,
Must break down these walls first, and then start anew.

For it's in the breaking, that beauty resides,
Butterfly emerging from its own cocoon,
That takes a leap of faith and through the air glides,
I too shall spread my wings and will break free soon.

Growing pains I embrace, though unsettled still,
Obstacles I can face, one step at a time,
I make sure to train hard, to strengthen my will,
For I know before flight, there must come a climb.

So I trust the process, transformed heart and mind,
On my way to become, who I'm meant to be,
For it's in the breakdown, my breakthrough I find,
And now emerge stronger, more vibrant and free.

Into the winds of change, full of trust I leap,
As I walk this pathway of continued growth.
No longer paralysed, my word I will keep,
To follow when needed my heart and mind both.

And when I finally spread my wings, take flight,
I'll soar so much higher, than thought possible.
No more caterpillar, lovely butterfly,
Embracing the journey, now unstoppable.

LESSONS LEARNED (FORGIVE YOURSELF)

In shadows of past, where regrets reside,
We often dwell on the tears that we've cried,
Moments we faltered, ignorant mistakes.
It's time to let go, new memories make.

Forgive yourself for what you didn't know,
Before you learnt it, you need time to grow.
Each stumble and fall, wrongly taken turn,
Led to this moment, wisdom must be learnt.

Review lessons learned, the knowledge you gained,
See how far you've come, and how much has changed.
But amidst despair, kindly soothe your mind,
As you must journey, for wisdom to find.

So forgive what was, the mistakes you've made,
You'll be empowered for what lies ahead.
With every hurdle, treat yourself with grace.
Beauty's in reprieve, in finding your place.

Let go of the guilt, let go of the pain,
And forgive yourself, you are not to blame.
For when you do so, your spirit's set free,
To soar to new heights, who you're meant to be.

Remember, dear friend, as you go on through,
That at that time you did not having a clue.
For wisdom comes with time and experience,
You know much more now, embrace your brilliance.

You're worthy of love, of joy and of light,
Free yourself of guilt so you can take flight.

AN ARROW

You need to pull backwards so arrows are shot.
Life yanking you rearward, you thought you got caught?
Acknowledge the tension, the pull of the bow,
Whose aim is to launch you, and to help you grow.

With each disappointment, each setback you face,
Life gets you equipped for the following race.
In the wake of battle, hardships you go through,
You gain the strength to soar, to rise and pursue.

Like an arrow pulled back, now ready to fly,
Life propels you forward, to reach for the sky.
With what seems like setbacks, you get closer still,
To the freedom of air, the triumphal thrill.

So embrace the challenge, the trials you face,
For they shape you, mold you, help you find your place.
An arrow to be shot must be drawn back first,
Then you're set in motion, in prospects immersed.

What You Thought You Can't Do

Not everyone has your best interest in mind,
No matter how gentle you are, or how kind,
A slight hesitation, they'll jump on the prey,
Do what they can do to make sure it's their way.

Not everyone wishes you well when you rise,
Jealous of your success, they envy your prize.
Seeds of doubt they will sow, try to dim your light,
So fearful of your shine, they'll act out of spite.

If you hear "it's too hard", "you can't", "you're too weak",
The best revenge for you, is find what you seek,
Use all your resources, all of your courage,
Be immune to those who try to discourage.

For if you make effort, truly try your best,
No doubt you'll accomplish your targeted quest.
The best satisfaction, that feeling so true,
Is through achieving what you thought you can't do.